Sichtungsgarten | Trial Garden
WEIHENSTEPHAN

Sichtungsgarten | Trial Garden

WEIHENSTEPHAN

Fotos | photos: Christa Brand
Texte | text: Bernd Hertle

Ulmer

EINFÜHRUNG

INTRODUCTION

Weihenstephan – ursprünglich Kloster, heute Ortsteil von Freising und eines der größten „grünen“ Wissenschaftszentren Europas – steht für Tradition und Moderne. „Bier“ und „Gärten“ sind Aushängeschilder, welche weit über die Grenzen Bayerns hinaus strahlen. Die von einem engagierten Team gepflegten Weihenstephaner Gärten sind Teil der Hochschule Weihenstephan-Triesdorf. Als ehemaliger Klostergarten kann der auf dem Weihenstephaner Berg gelegene Hofgarten auf eine jahrhundertelange Tradition zurückblicken. Der östlich benachbarte Oberdieckgarten entstand in den 1920er Jahren. Der 1947 gegründete, etwas über 5 ha große Sichtungsgarten ist somit keinesfalls der älteste, wohl aber der renommierteste der Weihenstephaner Gärten. An ihn grenzt der Kleingarten an, der Gemüse und Obst beherbergt.

ENTSTEHUNG UND ENTWICKLUNG DES GARTENS

Bereits um 1920 forderte der berühmte Staudengärtner und -züchter Karl Foerster eine zentrale Stelle zur Sichtung von Stauden. Erste Ansätze zur Errichtung von Sichtungsgärten machte jedoch der Krieg zunichte. Richard Hansen, der in seinen Wanderjahren von 1935 bis 1936 als

Weihenstephan – a former monastery today a district of Freising and one of the largest “green” science centres in Europe – stands for tradition and modernity. “Beer” and “gardens” are flagships reaching far beyond the borders of Bavaria. The Weihenstephan Gardens are part of the University of applied sciences and are looked after by a team of dedicated gardeners. As a former monastery garden, the Court Garden situated on the Weihenstephan hill can look back on a tradition of many centuries. The neighbouring Oberdieck Garden lying to the east of the court garden came into existence in the 1920s. The 5 ha Trial Garden founded in 1947 is therefore by no means the oldest one, it is, however, the most famous of the Weihenstephan Gardens. It borders on the garden plot producing fruit and vegetables.

CREATION AND DEVELOPMENT OF THE GARDEN

As early as 1920, the famous gardener and breeder of perennial plants, Karl Foerster, called for a central point for trailing perennials. But the first attempts to create trial gardens were destroyed by the war.

Eine robuste Stauden-Sonnenblume (*Helianthus* 'Lemon Queen') verschleiert den Blick auf das Gebäude mit Hörsaal, Büros, Werktrakt und Sozialräumen für Gärtner. | A robust *Helianthus* 'Lemon Queen' conceals the building which accommodates the lecture hall, offices, the workshop and staff facilities for the gardeners.

Gärtner bei Foerster in Bornim arbeitete, griff die Idee seines Lehrers auf, als er 1947 an die damalige Staatliche Lehr- und Forschungsanstalt berufen wurde und begann mit dem Aufbau des Sichtungsgartens. „Sichtung bedeutet Auslese der besten Züchtungen und der kulturwürdigen Arten, aber auch – unlösbar mit der Sichtung verbunden – das Erfassen des rechten Pflanzplatzes für jegliche Pflanze und damit, vor allem ökologisch betrachtet, geeigneter Partner und Nachbarn für gute Vergemeinschaftungen am Pflanzort“. Die von Hansen formulierte Aufgabenstellung prägt den Garten bis heute. Gärtnerische Pflanzengemeinschaften nach Vorbildern in der Natur sowie zur Beurteilung ihres Verwendungswerts aufgepflanzte Stauden- und

Richard Hansen who worked as a gardener for Foerster in Bornim during his years of travel from 1935–36, picked up his teacher's idea when he was appointed to the then National Teaching and Research Institute Weihenstephan and subsequently started to build on the Weihenstephan Trial Garden.

"Trialing means choosing the best cultivars and the species worth cultivating, but also – intrinsically tied to trialing – the determination of the best position for any plant and consequently, above all from an ecological point of view: suitable partners and neighbours should lead to thriving plant communities in that position". These instructions phrased by Hansen have an

Gehölzsortimente begegnen den Besuchern an vielen Stellen des Gartens. Dazu gesellen sich prachtvolle und neuartige Pflanzenarrangements, von denen viele unter der Ägide Peter Kiermeiers entstanden, der Hansen 1978 nachfolgte und den Garten bis 2006 leitete. Der Sichtungsgarten ist stets ein Lehr- und Versuchsgarten geblieben, in dem Studenten der Weihenstephaner Hochschulen ein breites Potpourri an Pflanzen und deren stimmige Verwendung kennenlernen können. Seine Pflanzungen, die auf Ökologie und Ästhetik basieren, laden Fachpublikum und interessierte Laien ein, sich intensiv mit der Verwendung von Gehölzen, Stauden und Sommerblumen auseinanderzusetzen oder schlicht die Schönheit des Gartens mit allen Sinnen zu genießen.

STANDÖRTLICHE VORAUSSETZUNGEN

Der Sichtungsgarten liegt etwa 470 m über dem Meeresspiegel in Winterhärtezone 6 a mit durchschnittlichen Jahrestiefsttemperaturen zwischen −20° und −23° C. Auch wenn die letzten Winter milder ausfielen, ist keine Kultur frostempfindlicher Pflanzen möglich. Wärmeliebende Gehölze wie *Cercis siliquastrum* oder *Viburnum tinus* überleben allenfalls an kleinklimatisch begünstigten Standorten. Wechselhaftes Winterwetter, in dem kalte Perioden von warmen Föhnwetterlagen unterbrochen werden und Temperaturunterschiede von über 20° C bringen, ist ein weiterer Auslesefaktor. Dazu gesellt sich ein schluffig lehmiger Boden, unter dem oft tonige Verdichtungshorizonte lagern, sodass nässeempfindliche Pflanzen in feuchten Wintern leiden. Stärkere Niederschläge lassen keine Bearbeitung der Flächen zu. In Trockenperioden verfestigt sich das sonst fruchtbare Erdreich rasch und neigt zu ausgeprägter Rissbildung. Bei einer Durchschnittstemperatur von 8,1° C fallen 792 mm Niederschläge im Jahr.

impact on gardens to this day. Plant communities in gardens using nature as a model as well as plantations of selected perennials and shrubs to determine their usability can be perceived by the visitors on many occasions as they stroll through the garden. Visitors can also admire magnificent plant arrangements, many of them created under the aegis of Peter Kiermeier who succeeded Hansen in 1978 and was in charge of the garden until 2006. The garden has always remained an educational and experimental garden allowing students of the Weihenstephan Universities to become acquainted with a large potpourri of plants and the conditions in which they are most likely to thrive. Its plantations, based on ecological aspects and aesthetics, attract experts as well as interested lay persons who want to learn in detail about the use of shrubs, perennials and annuals or simply enjoy the beauty of the garden.

HABITAT CONDITIONS

The Trial Garden is about 470 m above sea level in hardiness zone 6 a with average annual minimum temperatures between −20° and −23° C. Thermophile trees and shrubs such as *Cercis siliquastrum* or *Viburnum tinus* will at best survive in microclimatic conditions. Unsettled winter weather with cold periods interrupted by warm winds, so-called alpine foehn, causing differences in temperature of over 20° C is another selective factor. This is accompanied by a silty, loamy soil often containing embedded clay pans, so that plants sensitive to moisture suffer in humid winters. Heavier rainfall makes soil cultivation very difficult. During a drought period the otherwise fertile soil will rapidly harden and be prone to fracturing. The average yearly temperature is 8.1° C and the annual precipitation is 792 mm.

Blick vom Eingangsbereich über Akeleien (*Aquilegia vulgaris*), Kugel-Lauch (*Allium* 'Purple Sensation') und Tulpen (*Tulipa*) auf den Weihenstephaner Berg. | View from the entrance to the Weihenstephan hill overlooking *Aquilegia vulgaris, Allium* 'Purple Sensation' and *Tulipa*.

GLIEDERUNG DES GARTENS

Der Sichtungsgarten wird von einem Gehölzgürtel gerahmt. Erste Pflanzungen dafür wurden im östlichen Bereich ab 1948, im westlichen ab 1953 durchgeführt. Den Innenbereich des Gartens gliedern zurückhaltend eingesetzte Solitärgehölze und Hecken. Es verbleiben vorwiegend sonnige Flächen, die durch geradlinig verlaufende Rasenwege erschlossen sind. Die mittig gelegenen Flächen sind nur leicht geneigt, während sich nach Süden ein stärker abfallendes Areal anschließt. Auf diesen Flächen finden trockenheitsverträgliche Freiflächenstauden einen zusagenden Standort. Im östlichen Bereich noch stärker mit Zuchtformen kombiniert und gestalterisch arrangiert, nimmt der Anteil an Wildstauden nach Westen vom Kniphofia- über den Potentilla-Hang zur Steppenheide zu. Weiter westlich schließt sich der Steingarten an, bevor Gehölze die Szenerie dominieren. In ihrem Umfeld sind Stauden der Lebensbereiche Gehölz und Gehölzrand sowie zahlreiche Frühlingsgeophyten angesiedelt. Die inselartig dazwischen liegenden Sonnenflächen werden vornehmlich als Flächen für die Sichtung von Stauden und Gehölzen genutzt.

STRUCTURE OF THE GARDEN

The Trial Garden is framed by a belt of trees and shrubs. The first of these plants were established in 1948 in the eastern and in 1953 in the western side of the garden. The inner area is structured by means of some specimen trees and individual hedges. The remaining garden consists mainly of sunny areas with intersecting straight grass paths. While the areas in the middle of the garden are only gently sloped, the plot to the south is much steeper. This is an ideal area for drought-tolerant perennial plants preferring an open sunny position. In the eastern section there are some wild perennials, combined tastefully mainly with cultivars. Their number increases going westwards from the Kniphofia slope over the Potentilla slope to the steppe area. The rock garden is located further to the west. Then trees and shrubs dominate the scenery. They are surrounded by perennials belonging to the garden habitats "woodland" and "woodland edge" as well as numerous spring geophytes. This area is interspersed with sunny spots, mainly used for the shrubs and perennials trials.

DER SICHTUNGSGARTEN

1 Beete um Wasserbecken
2 Pastellbeete
3 Purpurbeete
4 Iris-sibirica-Beete
5 Gehölz und Gehölzrand
6 Pflanzungen in Violett-Gelb-Purpur
7 Wassergarten
8 Storchschnabel-Hang
9 Kniphofia-Hang
10 Rote Rabatte
11 Offener Gehölzrand
12 Pfingstrosen-Beete
13 Iris-germanica-Beete
14 Chinaschilf und Sommerflor
15 Potentilla-Hang
16 Steppenheide
17 Steingarten
18 BdS-Rabatte
19 Gelbes Quartier
20 Taglilien-Beete
21 Astilben-Pflanzung
22 Eichenquartier
23 Helle Rabatte
24 Frühlings- und Hosta-Weg
25 Haselquartier
26 Wildobstaboretum

THE TRIAL GARDEN

1 Beds around water basins
2 Pastel border
3 Purple border
4 Iris sibirica beds
5 Woodland and Woodland edge
6 Violet-yellow-purple beds
7 Water garden
8 Geranium slope
9 Kniphofia slope
10 Red border
11 Woodland edge
12 Paeonies
13 Iris germanica beds
14 Miscanthus and ornamentals
15 Potentilla slope
16 Steppe area
17 Rock garden
18 BdS border
19 Yellow corner
20 Daylilies
21 Astilbes
22 Oak corner
23 Pale border
24 Spring- and Hosta path
25 Hazel corner
26 Wild fruit arboretum

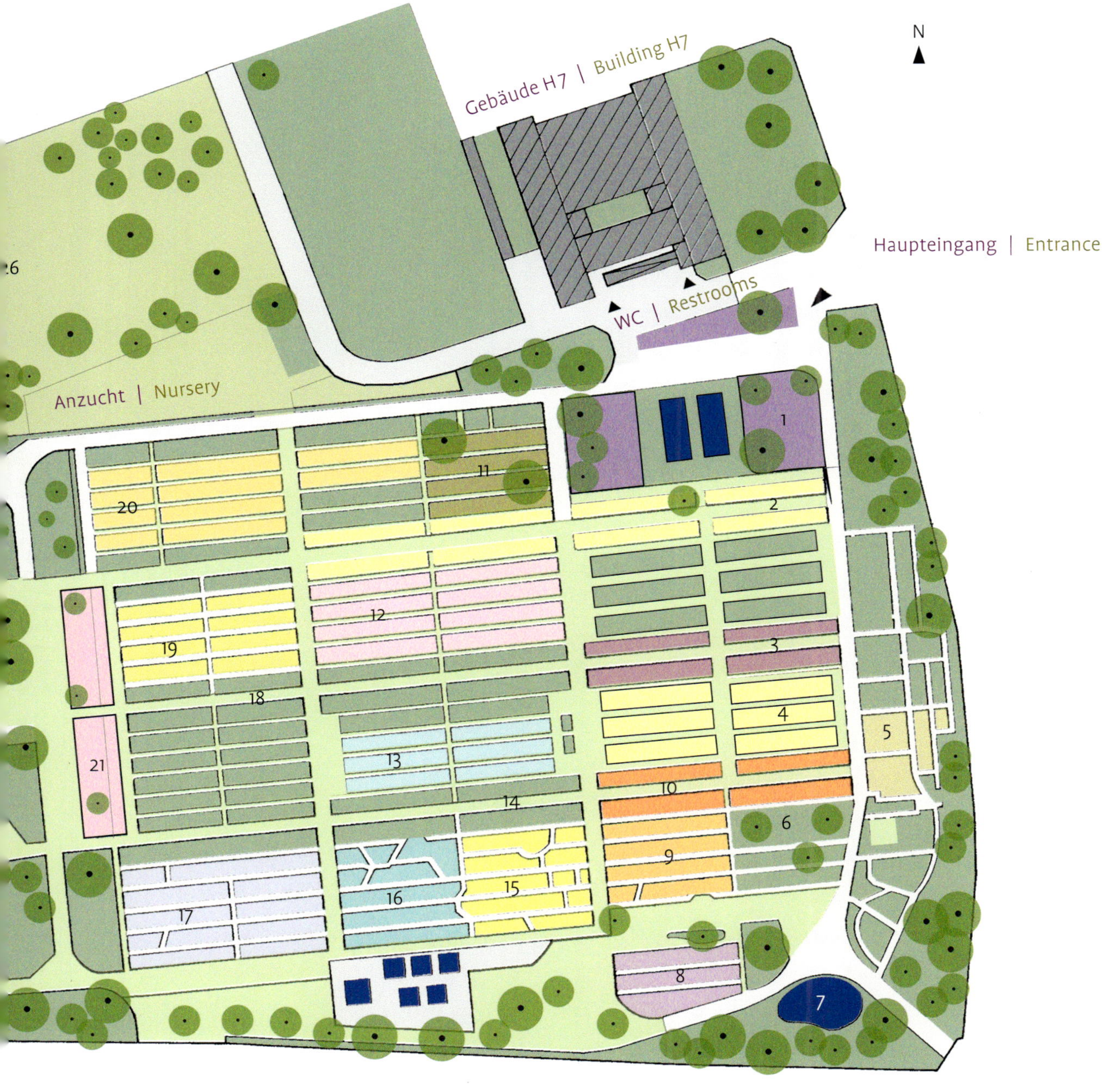

PRACHTVOLLE RABATTEN
SPLENDID BORDERS

Der Sichtungsgarten bietet gute Entwicklungsmöglichkeiten für Beetstauden, die einen frischen, gut mit Nährstoffen versorgten Standort lieben. Entlang der Hauptwege sind schmuckvolle Rabatten platziert. Mal sind es reine Staudenpflanzungen, mitunter „Mixed Borders“, in denen Gehölze wie Purpur-Perückenstrauch, Hibiskus oder Rosen mit Stauden und Einjährigen korrespondieren, und bisweilen bilden eindrucksvolle Großgräser das Rückgrat für ein Potpourri aus Sommerblumen. Neben bewährten Kombinationen entstehen jährlich neue Arrangements, denen unterschiedliche Farbkonzepte zugrunde liegen.

Flowering perennials that love a fresh, rich soil grow well in the Trial Garden. The main paths are lined with colourful flower beds. Some of the borders contain only perennials, some are mixed borders combining woody shrubs such as *Cotinus coggygria, Hibiscus* or roses with perennials and annuals and every now and then impressive tall grasses form the backbone of a summer flower potpourri. In addition to the established combinations, every year new arrangements are created, based on different colour designs.

Vorherige Seite: Das imposante Chinaschilf (*Miscanthus sinensis*) fällt im Herbst durch fedrige Rispen auf. Seine Sorten geben Sommerblumen einen schönen Rahmen. | Previous page: In autumn, the impressive *Miscanthus sinensis* develops silvery plumes. Its varieties make a beautiful frame for annuals.

Patagonisches Eisenkraut (*Verbena bonariensis*), Schmuckkörbchen (*Cosmos bipinnatus*), Spinnenblumen (*Cleome spinosa*), Löwenmäulchen (*Antirrhinum majus*) und Zinnien (*Zinnia elegans*) präsentieren sich in zarten Tönen. | *Verbena bonariensis, Cosmos bipinnatus, Cleome spinosa, Antirrhinum majus* and *Zinnia elegans* come in many shades of pastel colour.

Im Frühjahr bildet der Kugel-Lauch (*Allium* 'Ambassador') einen prägnanten Kontrast zu Gold-Liguster (*Ligustrum ovalifolium* 'Aureum') sowie Blut-Berberitzen (*Berberis thunbergii* 'Atropurpurea Nana'). Im Sommer (oben) übernehmen Duftnessel (*Agastache* 'Blue Fortune') und Kugeldisteln (*Echinops bannaticus* 'Taplow Blue') den blauen Part. | In spring, *Allium* 'Ambassador' provides a striking contrast to *Ligustrum ovalifolium* 'Aureum' and *Berberis thunbergii* 'Atropurpurea Nana'. In summer (top), *Agastache* 'Blue Fortune' and *Echinops bannaticus* 'Taplow Blue' take over the blue part.

Nächste Doppelseite: Steppen-Wolfsmilch (*Euphorbia seguieriana* subsp. *niciciana*) und Duftnessel (*Agastache* 'Blue Fortune') blühen bis in den frühen Herbst. | Following double page: *Euphorbia seguieriana* subsp. *niciciana*, and *Agastache* 'Blue Fortune' are in bloom until autumn.

Monochrome Farbverwendung in der Roten Rabatte: Blumenrohr (*Canna indica* 'Schwabenstolz') und Wunderbaum (*Ricinus communis* 'Carmencita Rot') setzen Akzente. | Use of monochromatic colours in the Red border: *Canna indica* 'Schwabenstolz' and *Ricinus communis* 'Carmencita Rot' add a particular touch.

Teufelsstrauch (*Physocarpus opulifolius* 'Diabolo') und Chinaschilf-Sorten (*Miscanthus sinensis*) bilden das dauerhafte Gerüst der Roten Rabatte. | *Physocarpus opulifolius* 'Diabolo' and *Miscanthus sinensis* form the permanent frame of the Red border.

Nächste Doppelseite: Sommerblumen wie Zinnien (*Zinnia elegans*), Dahlien (*Dahlia*) und einjährige Gräser (*Pennisetum villosum*) sorgen für jährlich wechselnde Bilder. | Following double page: Ornamentals such as *Zinnia elegans*, *Dahlia* and annual grasses (*Pennisetum villosum*) provide a changing display every year.

Purpurlaubige Perückensträucher (*Cotinus coggygria* 'Royal Purple') bilden den Grundstock der Purpurbeete. Ab Sommer haben hier Kurzlebige wie Patagonisches Eisenkraut (*Verbena bonariensis*) oder Prachtkerzen (*Gaura lindheimeri*) ihren Auftritt. | *Cotinus coggygria* 'Royal Purple' constitute the basis of the Purple border. In summer short-lived plants such as *Verbena bonariensis* or *Gaura lindheimeri* make their appearance.

Im Vorsommer komplettieren die Rosen 'Veilchenblau' und 'Mozart' sowie dauerhafte Bartfaden-Formen (*Penstemon digitalis* 'Husker's Red', *Penstemon hirsutus*), Pracht-Storchschnabel (*Geranium* × *magnificum*) und Purpurglöckchen (*Heuchera* 'Molly Bush') das Farbthema. | The early summer witnesses the colourful combination of the roses 'Veilchenblau' and 'Mozart' as well as the hardy *Penstemon digitalis* 'Husker's Red' and *Penstemon hirsutus*, *Geranium* × *magnificum* and *Heuchera* 'Molly Bush'.

Pastellbeete mit Gold-Hopfen (*Humulus lupulus* 'Aureus'), Stockrosen (*Alcea rugosa*), Taglilien (*Hemerocallis* 'Atlas') und Sommer-Margeriten (*Leucanthemum* 'Gruppenstolz'). | *Pastel border with Humulus lupulus* 'Aureus', *Alcea rugosa, Hemerocallis* 'Atlas' and *Leucanthemum* 'Gruppenstolz'.

Die Lilienblütigen Tulpen 'Westpoint' und 'White Triumphator' sowie Katzenminzen (*Nepeta racemosa* 'Superba') und Gold-Wolfsmilch (*Euphorbia polychroma*) bilden den Auftakt des Blütenreigens in den Pastellbeeten. | The Lily-flowered tulips 'Westpoint' and 'White Triumphator' as well as *Nepeta racemosa* 'Superba' and *Euphorbia polychroma* are the prelude to the marvellous floral display in the Pastel border.

In einer von Chinaschilf gegliederten Doppelrabatte entstehen durch Sommerblumen-Arrangements jährlich wechselnde Bilder. Mehl-Salbei (*Salvia farinacea*), Rotes Lampenputzergras (*Pennisetum setaceum* 'Rubrum'), Löwenmäulchen (*Antirrhinum majus*) und Sonnenhut (*Rudbeckia hirta*) erzeugen kontrastreiche Bilder. | Ornamental arrangements in a double flower bed structured by *Miscanthus sinensis* produce changing impressions from year to year. *Salvia farinacea, Pennisetum setaceum* 'Rubrum', *Antirrhinum majus* and *Rudbeckia hirta* create vivid contrasts.

Vorherige Doppelseite: Pultartige Staffelung: Höhere Formen wie Spinnenblumen (*Cleome spinosa*) oder Schmuckkörbchen (*Cosmos bipinnatus*) sind rückwärtig, niedrige Varianten wie Tagetes (*Tagetes patula*) weiter vorne platziert. | Previous double page: Staggered arrangement: Higher plants like *Cleome spinosa* or *Cosmos bipinnatus* are at the back, low-growing varieties like *Tagetes patula* at the front.

Einjährige finden stets einen Platz im Sichtungsgarten. Kaum eine andere Pflanzengruppe lässt ein abwechslungsreicheres Spiel mit Farben zu. Zier-Kohl (*Brassica oleracea* var. *acephala*), Zinnien (*Zinnia elegans*), Zier-Tabak (*Nicotiana sylvestris*), Spinnenblume (*Cleome spinosa*) und Eisenkraut (*Verbena rigida*) malen ein harmonisches Bild. | Annuals always find a place in the Trial Garden. There is hardly any other group of plants which shows a more diversified play of colours. *Brassica oleracea* var. *acephala*, *Zinnia elegans*, *Nicotiana sylvestris*, *Cleome spinosa* and *Verbena rigida* paint a harmonious arrangement.

Gleich ob mit Dahlien (*Dahlia*), Zinnien (*Zinnia angustifolia*) und Afrikanischem Lampenputzergras (*Pennisetum setaceum*) (links) oder einjährigen Sonnenhüten (*Rudbeckia hirta*) (rechts), die Blütenschirme des Bischofskrauts (*Ammi visnaga*) lassen sich auf vielfältige Weise gewinnbringend kombinieren. | The flower heads of *Ammi visnaga* can be beautifully combined in many different ways, be it with *Dahlia*, *Zinnia angustifolia* and *Pennisetum setaceum* (on the left) or the annual *Rudbeckia hirta* (on the right).

Im Frühling blühen auf der BdS-Rabatte, die anlässlich des 60. Jubiläums des Bundes deutscher Staudengärtner gepflanzt wurde, Gold- (*Euphorbia polychroma*) und Sumpf-Wolfsmilch (*Euphorbia palustris*) sowie einfache spätblühende Tulpen unter einem Zier-Apfel (*Malus toringo* var. *sargentii*), der im Herbst mit kleinen roten Äpfeln und gelbem Laub geschmückt ist. | In spring *Euphorbia polychroma*, *Euphorbia palustris* as well as single late tulips and *Malus toringo* var. *sargentii*, are flowering in the BdS border, which was created for the 60th anniversary of the Federation of German Perennial Plant Growers.

Im Herbst prägen Astern (*Aster novae-angliae* 'Violetta'), Goldrute (*Solidago rugosa* 'Fireworks'), Goldbartgras (*Sorghastrum nutans*) und Garten-Sandrohr (*Calamagrostis* x *acutiflora*) die BdS-Rabatte. | In autumn *Aster novae-angliae* 'Violetta', *Solidago rugosa* 'Fireworks', *Sorghastrum nutans* and *Calamagrostis* x *acutiflora* give distinction to the BdS border.

Im „Gelben Quartier“ gedeihen Prachtstauden, deren Eltern aus Nordamerika stammen. Im Sommer dominieren die warmen Farben von Sonnenbraut (*Helenium* 'Baudirektor Linne'), Goldrute (*Solidago* 'Goldstrahl') und Sonnenhut (*Rudbeckia fulgida* 'Goldsturm'). | In the "Yellow corner", cultivars of perennials whose parent plants are native in North America thrive well. The warm colours of *Helenium* 'Baudirektor Linne', *Solidago* 'Goldstrahl' and *Rudbeckia fulgida* 'Goldsturm' are predominant in summer.

Hochwüchsige Stauden wie die Sonnenbraut-Sorten 'Kugelsonne' oder 'Königstiger', Goldruten (*Solidago*) und Schlitzblättriger Sonnenhut (*Rudbeckia laciniata*) behaupten ihren Platz bereits seit vielen Jahren. | Tall, vigorous perennials such as *Helenium* 'Kugelsonne' and *Helenium* 'Königstiger', *Solidago* or *Rudbeckia laciniata* have been holding their ground for many years.

Vor nachtgrünen Koniferen bringen Geißbart (*Aruncus* 'Horatio'), Weißer Sommer-Salbei (*Salvia nemorosa* 'Adrian') und Weißbuntes Chinaschilf (*Miscanthus sinensis* 'Variegatus') Licht ins Dunkel. | *Aruncus* 'Horatio', *Salvia nemorosa* 'Adrian' and *Miscanthus sinensis* 'Variegatus' brighten the backdrop of dark green conifers.

Das Farbkonzept der Hellen Rabatte wird im Frühling bereits durch Sumpf-Wolfsmilch (*Euphorbia palustris*) und die Viridiflora-Tulpe 'Spring Green' – eine der wenigen langlebigen Tulpen im Sichtungsgarten – angedeutet. | In spring, the colour design of the Pale border already becomes apparent with *Euphorbia palustris* and *Tulipa* 'Spring Green' – one of the few long-lived tulips in the trial garden.

Die Kombination von Kissen-Astern mit Formen der Kupfer-Hirse (*Panicum virgatum*) ist beinahe schon ein Klassiker im Sichtungsgarten. Schon vor mehreren Jahrzehnten war die bewährte Zusammenstellung an anderer Stelle gepflanzt. | The combination of Aster Dumosus-Group with species of *Panicum virgatum* is virtually a classic in the Trial Garden. Many decades ago, the successful combination already thrived at a different spot.

Vorherige Doppelseite: Die auffällige Färbung des Laubs vieler Gehölze und Stauden ist nicht der einzige Höhepunkt im Herbst. Zahlreiche Gräser zeigen sich dann von ihrer schönsten Seite. | Previous double page: The colourful autumn leaves of many trees, shrubs and perennials are not the only highlight of that season. Many grasses are at their most beautiful in autumn.

Während ältere Züchtungen des Chinaschilfs (*Miscanthus*) wie 'Variegatus' im Sichtungsgarten kaum zur Blüte kommen, blühen Sorten wie 'Sirene' und 'Malepartus' sicher. Alle treiben spät aus, wachsen dann aber rasch zu meist übermannshohen Gestalten heran. | While older cultivars of *Miscanthus* such as 'Variegatus' are hardly ever in bloom in the Trial Garden, cultivars such as 'Sirene' and 'Malepartus' do not fail to bloom. All of them are late bloomers, but then they grow fast to over two metres.

PFLANZUNGEN AUF SÜDGENEIGTEN FLÄCHEN

PLANTATIONS ON SOUTHERN SLOPES

Die bindigen, gut Wasser haltenden Böden des Sichtungsgartens erschweren die Kultur nässeempfindlicher Pflanzen. Ein rascherer Wasserabzug und intensivere Sonneneinstrahlung bieten Stauden trockener Freiflächen bessere Bedingungen, sodass das natürliche Vorbild einer Steppenheide im südlichen Bereich gärtnerisch interpretiert wird, wo das Gelände stärker geneigt ist. Die Pflanzung enthält vornehmlich Wildstauden. Nach Osten schließen sich Potentilla- und Kniphofia-Hang an. Sie beherbergen – wie die weiter nördlich gelegenen Iris-germanica-Beete – neben Arten des Lebensbereichs Freifläche auch Zuchtformen und stellen einen Übergang zum trockenen Beet dar.

The heavy soil, able to retain water very easily, makes it difficult to cultivate moisture-sensitive plants. A faster draining soil and increased sunlight constitute better growing conditions for perennials occurring in arid open ground, so that the natural characteristics of steppe area recreated in the steeper slope of the southern part of the garden. The plantation consists mainly of wild forms. Potentilla and Kniphofia slopes are located in the east. Like the Iris germanica beds further north, they contain species from the garden habitat "open ground" as well as cultivated varieties and constitute a transition to the arid flower bed.

Vielfalt auf kleinem Raum: Orientalisches Lampenputzergras (*Pennisetum orientale*), Mexikanisches Federgras (*Nasella tenuissima*), Fetthenne (*Sedum* 'Matrona') und Kugelkopf-Lauch (*Allium sphaerocephalon*) in der Steppenheide. | Great diversity in a small area: *Pennisetum orientale, Nasella tenuissima, Sedum* 'Matrona' and *Allium* sphaerocephalon in the steppe area.

Vorherige Doppelseite: Kniphofia-Hang mit Steppenkerzen (*Eremurus himalaicus*), Junkerlilien (*Asphodeline lutea*), Kleinem Mädesüß (*Filipendula vulgaris*) und Feuer-Wolfsmilch (*Euphorbia griffithii* 'Fire Glow'). | Previous double page: *Kniphofia* slope with *Eremurus himalaicus, Asphodeline lutea, Filipendula vulgaris and Euphorbia griffithii* 'Fire Glow'.

Namensgebend für den Kniphofia-Hang sind zahlreiche Fackellilien. Im Sommer kontrastieren winterharte Montbretien 'Lucifer', Färberkamille (*Anthemis tinctoria*) und Knollige Seidenpflanze (*Asclepias tuberosa*) mit Blauraute (*Perovskia atriplicifolia*) und Schmucklilie (*Agapanthus campanulatus* subsp. *patens*) | The Kniphofia slope derives its name from this member of the lily family. In summer, the hardy *Crocosmia* 'Lucifer', *Anthemis tinctoria* and *Asclepias tuberosa* make a bold contrast to *Perovskia atriplicifolia* and *Agapantus campanulatus* subsp. *patens*.

In der Steppenheide geizen Spanischer Ginster (*Genista hispanica*) und Farnblättrige Pfingstrose (*Paeonia × smouthii*), eine Hybride aus Chinesischer (*Paeonia lactiflora*) und Netzblatt-Pfingstrose (*Paeonia tenuifolia*), nicht mit Farbe. Küchenschellen (*Pulsatilla vulgaris*) hingegen entwickeln bereits ihre fedrigen Samenstände. | In the steppe area, the colours of *Genista hispanica* and *Paeonia × smouthii*, a hybrid of *Paeonia lactiflora* and *Paeonia tenuifolia*, are impressive whereas *Pulsatilla vulgaris* already develops its feathery seed heads.

Vorherige Doppelseite: Ausdrucksstarke Wuchscharaktere von Atlas-Schwingel *(Festuca mairei)*, Riesen-Schuppenkopf (*Cephalaria gigantea)* und Königskerzen *(Verbascum chaixii)* zeichnen ein lebhaftes Bild im sommerlichen Potentilla-Hang. | Previous double page: The expressive growth of *Festuca mairei, Cephalaria gigantea* and *Verbascum chaixii* conveys a lively impression on the Potentilla slope in summer.

Veränderungen im Erscheinungsbild sind nicht nur jahreszeitlich bedingt. Königskerzen (*Verbascum olympicum*), Elfenbeindisteln (*Eryngium giganteum*) oder Rasselblumen (*Catananche caerulea*) vagabundieren stark, während Rotblättrige Berberitze (*Berberis thunbergii* 'Atropurea Nana') und Palmlilien (*Yucca filamentosa*) Fixpunkte bilden. | Changes in the appearance are not only associated with the different seasons. *Verbascum olympicum*, *Eryngium giganteum* or *Catananche caerulea* are strongly vagrant, while *Berberis thunbergii* 'Atropurea Nana' and *Yucca filamentosa* retain their appearance.

Nächste Doppelseite: Den weichen, flauschigen Blütenwalzen des Orientalischen Lampenputzergrases (*Pennisetum orientale*) setzt der Kleine Mannstreu (*Eryngium planum*) klare grafische Strukturen entgegen. | Following double page: The soft, fluffy flower spikes of *Pennisetum orientale* contrast with the clear structures of *Eryngium planum*.

Die hohe Bart-Iris 'Sharskin' ist wüchsig und verströmt einen angenehmen Zitronenduft. | The tall *Iris* 'Sharskin' (Germanica-Group) is vigorous and has a pleasant lemon scent.

Der klassische Farbdreiklang in Blau-Gelb-Weiß stellt sich bereits zur Blütezeit der Bart-Iris ein. | The typical mix of the three colours blue, yellow and white appears with the blooming period of the bearded iris.

Begleitet von kurzlebigen Salbei-Formen (*Salvia sclarea, Salvia argentea*) verlängern Steppen-Iris (*Iris spuria* 'Connoisseur', *Iris orientalis* 'Frigia') die Blütezeit in den Iris-germanica-Beeten. | Along with the short-lived species *Salvia sclarea* and *Salvia argentea, Iris spuria* 'Connoisseur' and *Iris orientalis* 'Frigia' extend the blooming period of the Iris germanica beds.

Nächste Doppelseite: Palmlilien (*Yucca filamentosa*), Lavendel (*Lavandula angustifolia*) und Steppen-Wolfsmilch (*Euphorbia seguieriana*) blühen nach den Iris. | Following double page: *Yucca filamentosa, Lavandula angustifolia* and *Euphorbia seguieriana* bloom after the irises.

STEINGARTEN
ROCK GARDEN

Der terrassenartig angelegte Steingarten hat seinen Ursprung in den 1950er Jahren. Er ist überwiegend aus Kalkstein gebaut, doch finden sich in seinem westlichen Teil auch härtere Urgesteinsformen. Kleinräumig wird das architektonische Grundkonzept durch Partien ergänzt, die den Charakter eines natürlichen Felsensteingartens aufweisen. Der üppigste Flor stellt sich von Frühjahr bis Vorsommer ein. Die Fülle von Blaukissen, Steinkraut, Schleifenblumen, Enzianen (*Aubrieta*, *Aurinia saxatilis*, *Iberis*, *Gentiana*) und anderen bekannten Steingartensortimenten wird ergänzt durch kleinwüchsige Zwiebelpflanzen, einzelne Zwerggehölze und mancherlei Kleinod.

The terrassed rock garden originated in the 1950s. It is chiefly made out of limestone, however, harder forms of primary rocks can be found in the western part. Here and there, the basic architectural concept is enhanced with parts featuring the characteristics of a natural rock garden. From spring to early summer the blooming season is at its peak. The abundance of *Aubrieta, Aurinia saxatilis, Iberis, Gentiana* and other well-known rock garden plants is complemented by low-growing bulbs, single small shrubs and the odd plant treasure.

Pfingst-Nelken, Alpen-Astern, Steintäschel, Ehrenpreis (*Dianthus gratianopolitanus, Aster alpinus, Aethionema, Veronica*) – der Steingarten birgt viele reich blühende, oft polster- oder teppichartig wachsende Formen. | *Dianthus gratianopolitanus, Aster alpinus, Aethionema, Veronica* – the rock garden holds many profusely blooming species, often forming a cushion or covering the ground like a carpet.

EINE GLÜCKLICHE LIAISON
STAUDEN UND GEHÖLZE

A GOOD COMBINATION
PERENNIALS AND WOODY PLANTS

Schon zeitig im Jahr regt sich Leben unter Baum und Strauch. Vorfrühlingsgeophyten und Stauden des Lebensbereichs Gehölz nutzen die lichtreiche Zeit bis zum Laubaustrieb der Gehölze für frisches Ergrünen und eine oft verschwenderische Blütenfülle. Später ebbt der Farbreichtum ab. Die Szenerien im Hasel- und im Eichenquartier bieten dann ein reizvolles Spiel verschiedener Wuchsformen, Texturen und unterschiedlicher Grünschattierungen. Am Gehölzrand hingegen setzt sich der Staudenflor bis in den Herbst fort, um dann mit buntem Herbstlaub von Bäumen und Sträuchern für ein letztes Aufleuchten vor dem Winter zu sorgen.

Early in the year plants begin to grow on the ground beneath trees and shrubs. Spring geophytes and perennials belonging to the garden habitat "woodland" take advantage of the increasing sunlight until the beginning of shoot growth to produce fresh greenery and lavish blossoms. Later the richness in colour will diminish. The hazel and oak corners then depict a charming variety of plants with different growth forms, textures and diverse shades of green. On the woodland edge, however, the perennials bloom until autumn. Together with the autumn colour of woody plants they create a wonderful autumn scenery before the winter comes.

Der wüchsige Straußenfarn (*Matteuccia struthiopsis*) erobert sich mit Ausläufern ein größeres Areal unter einer gelb blühenden Rosskastanie (*Aesculus flava*). | The vigorous *Matteuccia struthiopsis* spreads by sending out stolons under the yellow flowering *Aesculus flava*.

Im Vorfrühling scheinen Balkan-Windröschen (*Anemone blanda*), Puschkinie (*Puschkinia scilloides* var. *linbanotica*), Schneestolz (*Chionodoxa sardensis*) und Blausternchen (*Scilla siberica*) unter einer Schwarz-Weide (*Salix myrsinifolia*) geradezu um die Wette zu blühen. | In early spring, *Anemone blanda*, *Puschkinia scilloides* var. *linbanotica*, *Chionodoxa sardensis* and *Scilla siberica* seem to want to outbloom each other under a *Salix myrsinifolia*.

Vorherige Doppelseite: Durch reiche Selbstaussaat bildet der aus Südost-Europa stammende Elfen-Krokus (*Crocus tommasinianus*) allmählich eindrucksvolle Blütenteppiche. | Previous double page: The self-seeding *Crocus tommasinianus* native to Southeast Europe gradually forms impressive flower carpets.

Im Westen des Gartens geben sich Dichter-Narzissen (*Narcissus poeticus* 'Actaea') unter Lärchen ein Stelldichein. Sie verströmen einen angenehmen Duft und eignen sich bestens zum Verwildern in Wiesen, die spät gemäht werden. | On the western side of the garden, *Narcissus poeticus* 'Actaea' seem to have gathered under some larches. They are pleasantly scented and best suited to run to seed in meadows which are mowed late in the year.

Die heimische Schachbrettblume (*Fritillaria meleagris*), auch Kiebitzei genannt, wächst in der Natur vornehmlich auf sonnigen Feuchtwiesen, fühlt sich jedoch im Sichtungsgarten in einem lichten Gehölzhain sichtlich wohl. | In the wild, the native *Fritillaria meleagris*, also known as the guinea-hen flower, favours sunny, wet meadows, but in the Trial Garden it feels very much at home in a sparse woodland.

Bereits ausgangs des Winters blüht das Vorfrühlings-Alpenveilchen (*Cyclamen coum*). Unter einer Schirm-Heckenkirsche (*Lonicera maackii*) hat die Art einen größeren Bestand gebildet. Später blühen hier viele andere Geophyten. | *Cyclamen coum* already blooms at the end of winter. This species has formed a large community under a *Lonicera maackii*. Later on many other geophytes will blossom here.

Nächste Doppelseite: Viele Storchschnabel-Formen werden nach der Blüte bodennah zurückgeschnitten. Nach Neuaustrieb bilden sie rasch wieder eine dichte Decke. | Following double page: Many types of *Geranium* are cut back close to ground level after flowering. Once they start sprouting they will rapidly form a thick carpet again.

Von den vielen Formen der Prachtspieren im Astilbenbeet blühen die Abkömmlinge von *Astilbe chinensis* erst im Spätsommer. Es sind langlebige und wüchsige Stauden, die Trockenphasen besser als andere Astilben überstehen. | The Astilbe flower bed features many varieties, of which *Astilbe chinensis* has flowers only in late summer. These perennials are long-lived and vigorous and tolerate dry spells better than other Astilbes.

Zusammen mit prächtig gefärbten Blättern von Blumen-Hartriegeln und braunen Fruchtständen von Astilben setzen Oktober-Silberkerze (*Actaea simplex* 'White Pearl') und Herbst-Eisenhut (*Aconitum carmichaelii* 'Spätlese') einen Schlussakkord im Astilbenbeet. | Together with the magnificently coloured leaves of *Cornus kousa* and brown Astilbe seed heads, the symphony of colour in the Astilbe flower bed is rounded off with *Actaea simplex* 'White Pearl' and *Aconitum carmichaelii* 'Spaetlese'.

Nächste Doppelseite: Nach frischem Austrieb und reichem Flor der Waldstauden sorgen Genter Azaleen (*Rhododendron* 'Pallas' und 'Coccinea Speciosa') im Eichenwald für Farbe und Duft. | Following double page: After the sprouting and full bloom of the perennials thriving best under trees and shrubs, *Rhododendron* 'Pallas' and '*Coccinea Speciosa*' bring colour and fragrance to the oak corner.

Im Frühling prägen Narzissen, Zier-Kirschen sowie die bunten Rinden von Hartriegeln und Weiden das Bild. Später säumen üppig entwickelte Herzblattlilien wie 'Green Acres' oder 'Frances Williams' (rechts) den Hosta-Weg. | Daffodils, flowering cherries as well as dogwood and willows with their striking bark colours unravel their beauty in the springtime. Later on, sumptuous Hostas like *Hosta* 'Green Acres' or *Hosta sieboldiana* 'Frances Williams' line the Hosta path.

Grazil und filigran erscheint der Neuaustrieb des Venushaarfarns (*Adiantum venustum*) unter einer Haselnuss (*Corylus avellana*). Der wintergrüne Farn ist jedoch zäher als man denkt und bildet mit kurzen Ausläufern dauerhafte Bestände. | The new shoots of *Adiantum venustum* under a *Corylus avellana* have a graceful and delicate appearance, but the wintergreen fern is tougher than it looks and forms permanent communities with short stolons.

Im Haselquartier finden Schaublätter (*Rodgersia podophylla* 'Rotlaub') unter dem Schirm von Gehölzen einen zusagenden Standort. Anfangs noch zurückhaltend, beanspruchen die spät austreibenden Blattschmuckpflanzen allmählich mehr Raum. | Protected by trees and shrubs, the hazel corner is a suitable location for *Rodgersia podophylla* 'Rotlaub'. Growing slowly at first, the late sprouting foliage plants gradually take up more space.

Nächste Doppelseite: Der sommergrüne *Rhododendron kaempferi* ist ein verlässlicher Blüher. Im Oktober bezaubert er mit leuchtend orangerotem Herbstlaub. | Following double page: The deciduous *Rhododendron kaempferi* is a reliable bloomer. In October, the bright red and orange autumn leaves are captivating.

Späte Oktoberstimmung: Ginkgo (*Ginkgo biloba*) im leuchtend goldgelben und Rotstieliger Streifen-Ahorn (*Acer capillipes*) im pfirsichfarbenen Herbstgewand mit noch grünen Kopfweiden. | Impressions in late October: *Ginkgo biloba* enchants with its bright golden yellow and *Acer capillipes* with its peach-coloured autumn foliage while the pollarded willows are still green.

Farbenfrohes Herbst-Ensemble, das Wärme ausstrahlt: Zaubernuss-Sorten (*Hamamelis × intermedia* 'Diane'), Eisenholz (*Parrotia persica*) und Blasenesche (*Koelreuteria paniculata*) mit letzten duftenden Blüten der Lilien-Funkie (*Hosta plantaginea*). | Colourful autumn scenery radiating warmth: *Hamamelis × intermedia* 'Diane', *Parrotia persica* and *Koelreuteria paniculata* with *Hosta plantaginea*'s last fragrant flowers.

FEUCHTE BEETE UND WASSER

MOIST OPEN GROUND AND WATER

Boden- und Klimabedingungen erleichtern die Kultur feuchtigkeitsliebender Stauden im Sichtungsgarten. In den Iris-sibirica-Beeten gewährleisten Tropfbewässerung und Mulch, dass die Pflanzen in niederschlagsarmen Perioden ausreichend mit Wasser versorgt bleiben. Hier gedeihen vornehmlich Arten, die aus Feuchtwiesen stammen, sowie deren Zuchtformen. Die Pflanzung bildet einen Übergang vom Lebensbereich feuchte Freifläche zum Beet ab. Stauden der Lebensbereiche Wasserrand und Wasser sind um und in einem Teich sowie in mehreren Wasserbecken angesiedelt.

Soil and climatic conditions facilitate the culture of moisture-loving perennials in the Trial Garden. Drip irrigation and mulch in the Iris sibirica flower beds ensure that the plants continuously obtain sufficient water in periods of low rainfall. Mainly species native to wet meadows as well as their cultivated varieties thrive here. The plantation represents a transition from the garden habitat “moist open ground” to the border. Perennials native to the garden habitats “water’s edge” and “water” were planted in and around a pond as well as in several water basins.

Edel präsentiert sich die Wiesen-Iris (*Iris sibirica* ‘Caesar‘s Brother’) in der Partnerschaft mit Chinesischer Trollblume (*Trollius chinensis* ‘Golden Queen’) und Weißer Himmelsleiter (*Polemonium caeruleum* ‘Album’) | The natural elegance and grace of *Iris sibirica* ‘Caesar’s Brother’ associate well with *Trollius chinensis* ‘Golden Queen’ and *Polemonium caeruleum* ‘Album’.

Eine dunkle Eiben-Kulisse (*Taxus baccata*) rahmt den Teich, in dem Teichsimse (*Schoenoplectus lacustris*), Seerosen (*Nymphaea*), Amerikanische Teichrose (*Nuphar advena*), Seekanne (*Nymphoides peltata*), Krebsschere (*Stratiotes aloides*), Schwertblättrige Binse (*Juncus ensifolius*) und viele andere Wasser- und Uferpflanzen in unterschiedlichen Wassertiefen wachsen. | *Schoenoplectus lacustris, Nymphaea, Nuphar advena, Nymphoides peltata, Stratiotes aloides, Juncus ensifolius* and many other water and bankside plants grow at different water depths in a pond framed by a dark backdrop of *Taxus baccata*.

Die Sorten der Wiesen-Iris (*Iris sibirica*)'Caesar's Brother'und 'Weißer Orient' sowie die Sumpf-Wolfsmilch (*Euphorbia palustris*) bilden zur Blütezeit einen spannenden Dreiklang. Im Herbst leuchtet ihr Laub in warmen Gelb- und Orangetönen. |
During flowering, the varieties of *Iris sibirica* 'Caesar's Brother' and 'Weißer Orient' as well as *Euphorbia palustris* create an exciting triadic color scheme.

SICHTUNGEN
UND PFLANZENSAMMLUNGEN

TRIALS
AND PLANT COLLECTIONS

Für die Beurteilung des Gartenwerts sind Gehölz- und Staudensortimente aufgepflanzt. Dies gibt Besuchern die Möglichkeit, sich einen Überblick über die Formenvielfalt der jeweiligen Arten zu verschaffen und die Sorten vergleichend zu betrachten. Nach Abschluss der mehrjährigen Sichtung werden die Versuchsflächen geräumt. Dies bedingt einen raschen Wechsel in der Flächenbelegung. Frühere Sichtungen indes waren Basis für einige Pflanzensammlungen. Dabei wurde die Vielfalt älterer Taglilien durch neuere Formen erweitert, die Pfingstrosen durch Ergänzung von Pracht-Storchschnabel und Frauenmantel aufgewertet.

Assortments of trees, shrubs and perennials are planted for the evaluation of their garden merit. This allows visitors to discover and compare the many species and their varieties. After the trial period, which generally lasts a few years, the study site will be cleared. Thus, the areas are frequently replanted. However, plants from earlier trials were the basis of some plant collections. The diversity of older dayliliy cultivars was widened by introducing new varieties, Paeonies were enhanced by adding *Geranium × magnificum* and *Alchemilla mollis*.

Umspielt vom Schleier-Frauenmantel (*Alchemilla mollis*) präsentiert die Chinesische Pfingstrose (*Paeonia lactiflora* 'Le Cygne') ihre großen gefüllten Blüten. | Double-flowered *Paeonia lactiflora* 'Le Cygne' is surrounded by *Alchemilla mollis*.

Unter der Federführung des Bundessortenamts werden in Weihenstephan und anderen Standorten neben Rosenneuheiten umfangreiche Gehölzsortimente wie das der Rispen-Hortensien (*Hydrangea paniculata*) auf ihren Gartenwert geprüft. | Under the auspices of the Bundessortenamt new breeds of roses as well as a large selection of trees and shrubs like *Hydrangea paniculata* are evaluated as to their suitability for growing in gardens in Weihenstephan and other locations.

Vor der Prüfung von Staudensortimenten wird zunächst eruiert, ob die einzelnen Sorten richtig benannt sind. Wie bei den Kerzen-Knöterichen (*Bistorta amplexicaulis*) werden hierfür Pflanzen aus unterschiedlichen Gärtnereien bezogen und nebeneinander aufgepflanzt. | Before trialing different cultivars of perennial plants, a pre-trial shows if the cultivars, for example *Bistorta amplexicaulis*, sent from different leading perennial nurseries are correctly labeled.

Taglilien (*Hemerocallis*) sind sehr robuste und langlebige Gartenpflanzen. Die umfangreiche Sammlung bietet unter anderem einen Einblick in die Arbeit deutscher Züchter. | *Hemerocallis* are robust and long-lived bedding plants. The large collection reveals, among other things, an insight into the work of German breeders.

Die zweifarbige und großblütige Taglilien-Sorte 'Frans Hals' blüht im Hochsommer. Sie ist wenig anspruchsvoll und schon von weitem ein echter Hingucker. | The two-coloured and large-flowered *Hemerocallis* 'Frans Hals' blossoms in midsummer. It is low-maintenance and an eye-catcher from a distance.

KONTAKT

Hochschule Weihenstephan-Triesdorf
Am Staudengarten 7
85354 Freising
Deutschland

T 0049 8161 71-4026 (vormittags)
F 0049 8161 71-5596

gaerten@hswt.de
www.hswt.de/weihenstephaner-gaerten.html

ÖFFNUNGSZEITEN

1. April bis 31. Oktober, auch an Sonn- und Feiertagen
9:00 – 18:00 Uhr
Der Besuch der Gärten ist kostenlos.

ADRESS

University of Weihenstephan-Triesdorf
Am Staudengarten 7
85354 Freising
Germany

T 0049 8161 71-4026 (mornings)
F 0049 8161 71-5596

gaerten@hswt.de
www.hswt.de/weihenstephaner-gaerten.html

OPENING HOURS

April to October,
including weekends and public holidays
9:00 am – 6:00 pm
Admission to the garden ist free.

Vorherige Doppelseite: Die Blüte der Chinesischen Pfingstrosen (*Paeonia lactiflora*) ist ein Höhepunkt im Gartenjahr. Viele Sorten stehen hier seit den 1950er Jahren unverpflanzt. | Previous double page: The blossoms of *Paeonia lactiflora* are a highlight every year. Many varieties have not been transplanted since the 1950s.

IMPRESSUM

Bibliografische Information der Deutschen Nationalbibliothek
Die Deutsche Nationalbibliothek verzeichnet diese Publikation in der Deutschen Nationalbibliografie; detaillierte bibliografische Daten sind im Internet über http://dnb.d-nb.de abrufbar.

Wollgrasweg 41, 70599 Stuttgart (Hohenheim)
E-Mail: info@ulmer.de
Internet: www.ulmer.de
Übersetzung ins Englische:
Miriam Schmid/ade team übersetzungen
Lektorat: Claudia Ade/ade team übersetzungen, Helen Haas
Herstellung: Gabriele Wieczorek
Gartenplan: Hochschule Weihenstephan - Triesdrof
Umschlagentwurf: Katja v. Ruville, Frankfurt a. M.
Satz: Katja v. Ruville, Frankfurt a. M.
Reproduktion: timeRay Visualisierungen, Herrenberg
Druck und Bindung: Firmengruppe Appl, aprinta druck, Wemding
Printed in Germany

ISBN 978-3-8001-8298-5